IN HER SKIN
THE BLACK WOMAN

Daniella M. Butler

In Her Skin
The Black Woman
Daniella M. Butler

Butler, Daniella M.
In Her Skin: The Black Woman
www.DaniellaMButler.com
Email: info@daniellambutler.com

ISBN: 979-8-9921648-3-1 (Paperback)
ISBN: 979-8-9921648-4-8 (Hardcover)
ISBN: 979-8-9921648-5-5 (eBook)

Printed in the United States of America

First Edition: February 2025
Series: Unsilenced Voices

CONTENTS

This book is dedicated to
all the **Black Women** in my life.

The Shades of Me

A Rare Black Pearl

You say I'm pretty
For a dark skin girl,
As though it's a pity
I am a **Black Pearl**.

Oh, so should I be grateful
For your shock and surprise,
And dismiss your hateful
Complimental prize?

You say that I'm pretty
For a dark skin girl,
Implying it's a pity
That I'm a **Black Pearl**.

Oh, was I supposed to be ugly
And undeserving of love,
While being looked at smugly
By your gilded perched dove?

You say I'm pretty
For a dark skin girl,
Because you think it's a pity
That I'm a **Black Pearl**.

Oh, am I to be defined by you
And other dark skin girls,
Should let you define them too
And forget our value as black pearls?

You say that I'm pretty
For a dark skin girl,
But it's definitely not a pity
That I'm a beautiful, rare **Black Pearl**.

Not Your Superwoman

Tired and worn down,
Being called superwoman
Doesn't give me a crown.

A line to abuse me.
A line to keep on
Using me.
Not lifting a finger,
Your hand stretched out
In front of me.

Praising me
For not taking care
Of myself,
Because I'm too busy
Taking care of
Everyone's ungrateful self.

I'm not your superwoman,
I'm supposed to be
Your woman.
Lessening my load
Is how you show
You love this Black Woman.

Light-Skinned Privilege

Light-skinned privilege is knowing
That you have a chance of being accepted.
Light-skinned privilege means
Your darker sisters should be protected.

Yes, you have no control
Of the skin you were born in,
But you can be more empathized with
When you debate against the majority's sins.

Light-skinned privilege is knowing
That beauty is borderless.
It's not allowing racist mindsets
To make darker black women feel powerless.

Across the African continent,
They are different shades of black.
So, remember to use your light-skinned privilege
To protect your sister's back.

Commentaries on My Black Life

He said, "Nothing too black is ever good,"
That's because when they look at us
They see an escapee from the hood.

The darker we are
The more pushback we'll get.
It's a whirlwind of events to make us never forget.

She said, "Why are there still dark skin blacks?
Didn't we breed them out during slavery?
Oh! I can tell those neighbors' grandkids are black."

Since you think everyone with a drop of black
Is automatically full black,
Aren't you the one being bred out, you hateful hack?

She said, "Gotta lighten up and bleach my black skin
Cause nobody wants to see
This black woman win."

Destroying your beautiful melanin skin is a sin.
Giving yourself cancer,
Is never a win for your beautiful dark skin.

She said, "Hush, black babies need jobs too."
Dark skin babies can only play the infant roles,
For the adult versions are for light-skinned actors to do.

Either the movie industry has no black friends
Or they're purposely staying ignorant
To how dark skin babies look like as adults in the end.

He said, "Black women always fighting somebody."
Living in this world unprotected,
Must I allow them to attack my black body?

Stripped away my femininity
Because fiercely protecting my black self
Is viewed as masculinity.

My Eye Color Does Not Belong to You

I'm not wearing contacts to look like you.
Not mixed race or trying to take your place.
I had no eye surgery to make my eyes blue.
My eye color does not belong to your race.

I'm a human woman, just like you.
My eye color does not belong to you.

My skin remains a milk chocolate shade of brown.
And the hair on my head is a spiral of a coily crown.
My eye color is the same when I was born in my town,
So, stop looking at me with your scowl and frown.

I'm a human woman, just like you.
My eye color does not belong to you.

My African ex-husband said my blue eyes are sinister.
This white woman thinks I'm stealing her relevance.
Everywhere I go, judgment is ministered,
For judgment of the black woman is prevalent.

I'm a human woman, just like you.
My eye color does not belong to you.

Vanilla Is Brown

Yes, vanilla is clearly brown,
So, no one was trying to take your crown.
I wasn't describing vanilla ice cream
For that turned pale in the 1920s, it seems.

Yes, a black woman's color can be vanilla,
So, no one was stealing your skin tone, Priscilla.
Take a look at the vanilla bean,
Now tell me what color can clearly be seen.

Yes, vanilla is clearly brown,
So, stop trying to chase me out of town.
Why are you behaving like a hateful clown?
Screaming won't make your opinions renowned.

Yes, a black woman's color can be vanilla,
So, please calm yourself down, Priscilla.
Mind your business and get out of my face,
And stop constantly breaking into my safe space.

Color of My Blackness

You say I'm not dark enough
To speak on the Black Diaspora.
Pointing out my pigment
Against your medium-dark melanin skin.

The color of my blackness
Is not determined by you.
Because according to my DNA,
I'm blacker than you.

You say I'm not old enough
To tell our black story.
Pointing out my age
Against your worn, tired face.

The age of my blackness
Is not determined by you.
You lived your whole life hiding
Instead of battling against false truths.

You say my hair is not kinky enough
To speak on the black hair journey.
Pointing out that my coils
Are looser than your naps.

The status of my natural hair
Is not determined by you.
Your hair would look like mine
If you moisturized your dry hair too.

All this fight against someone
Who wants us all to win.
You're like a crab in a barrel
Pulling us into the abyss to sink.

The Hybrid Child

I see myself as mixed race;
A hybrid of two luxury styles into one space.
But if I'm asked to pick a side,
I will choose black with the utmost pride.

For society already sees me as black;
Asexual birth to my black parent's DNA sac.
So, if you attack the black side of me,
One hundred percent black woman I'll be.

So, although I know I'm a hybrid child,
Black is the default our society has filed.
Excluded from my white half in this nation,
I proudly accept this honor to my black station.

So Much Melanin in Her Skin

So much melanin in her skin,
The whites of her eyes darken from within.
Casting a protective shield from the bright sun,
This tinted brown is in nature's daughters and sons.

So much melanin in her skin,
Forming a protective sunscreen from within.
With this natural protection from the harsh sun,
A youthful, natural glow when proper care is done.

So much melanin in her skin,
Higher mineral, denser bones from within.
A test may say she's deficient in vitamin D,
But Black people have stronger bones; studies agree.

So much melanin in her skin,
Lightening it with cream is a cancerous sin.
Removed herself from places with "Black weathering,"
And fixed her mindset to protect her magical melanin.

Coils of My Hair

Magical Coily Hair

Spiraling upwards towards the sky,
Knowing no boundaries as it aims high.
Rooted in African spiritual head,
When matted, locs referred to as dread.

Threading of coils around each other,
Happily playing as sisters and brothers.
Coming together to unite as one
Spiral of hair rising towards the sun.

Chemically burned a part by hate,
Destruction of kinks to becoming straight.
Curse placed in now non-spiritual minds,
To remove the magical coily shrine.

Spiraling upwards towards the sky,
Knowing no boundaries as it aims high.
Remove the kinks that dwell in your head
And save your beautiful coils instead.

Let Your Locs Down Low

Let your beautiful locs down low.
Through your entity, ancestors flow.
Forming unity that casts a glow.
And making your spirit free to grow.

Samson up your locs with your strength.
Continue to grow it longer in length.
Don't cut it off despite hate or fright.
Use all your strength to win the fight.

Let your beautiful locs down low,
Swaying with it as the wind blows.
While you're caring for it like a pro,
You'll gain benefits from what you sow.

Slave Hair Catcher

Sis, why are you shaming me
For my tighter coils?
Speaking all proudly,
With your belittling voice.

Telling me, "My curls
Are much looser than yours,"
While you're wearing
A creamy crack hairstyle.
Makes you a slave hair catcher.

Even if your coils
Are looser than mine
Must you plague me
With your slavery mind?

Not so long ago
Black hair was, "Slave hair."
Wanting to fit in,
We "relaxed" it straight.
In return, we got fibroids and cancer.

"Those with nappy hair
Shouldn't go natural."
Thanks for the commentary,
Oh, faithful slave hair catcher.

I set my hair free
From corporate America
And the military.
Oh, and lest we forget you,
Ole slave hair catchers.

Black Hair Hate

Hide your daughter from black hair hate.
Protect her confidence like a gate.
Don't leave her with Grandma Faith.
For she believes, "Nappy hair should be straight."

Her grandmas, her aunties, her stepmom too,
All want to put their hair insecurities on you.
Belittling you for not straightening her hair,
Making you out to be a mother who doesn't care.

Hide your daughter from black hair hate.
Protect her confidence like a gate.
Stepmom plans to relax your daughter's hair,
Feeling protected because Daddy doesn't care.

Did they care when you yelled some threats?
Use the system to prevent regrets.
To protect your daughter from slavery minds,
Supervise their visits to stop hair hate crimes.

Hair Murderers

Some of you are running wild,
With your tight protective hairstyles.
If they're snatching the roots up off your head,
Best believe your strands will be dead.

If you have to sleep on your face
Your scalp hurts as the hair tightens your face.
Best believe hair death is imminent
For your strands will be eliminated.

Though a protective style is good haircare
For most type 4 natural hair.
Alopecia will be your best friend
If you wear tight hairstyles in the end.

Wash Hair Day

Wash Hair Day is a day,
We type 4 hair, black sisters wash our hair.
So don't make any instant plans
Or invite us anywhere.

Don't tell me
I have ten minutes to get ready,
Because you'll get cussed out
Like Uncle Eddie.

Wash Hair Day followed by styling
Is a day's journey.
So don't mess with my process
Or I'll have to get an attorney.

Don't judge me
Because your white hair is not like mine.
Or compare my coils
To straight hair during this time.

Wash Hair Day is a day,
We 4-type hair black sisters wash our hair.
So don't force any last-minute plans on us
Because today is my day to wash my hair.

Girls With Curls

I'm having a love affair with my curls
Because today they're very good girls.
Bouncing around and being juicy cute,
While uniformly lying flat at the roots.

Gotta show them off to the whole world.
Look, they're all making perfect little swirls.
Wearing a dress to match my black girl curves,
I went outside showing them the love they deserve.

As soon as the humidity hit my voluminous curls,
They shrank to my head and now I'm a TWA girl.
Sometimes each curl reminds me of a child!
I gotta put them in braids because they're being wild.

Black Hair Salons

It's much more than doing our hair,
For it's a community of sisterhood who cares.
A place of sanctuary, a place to unwind,
This is how black hair salons are defined.

Because of the uniqueness of our hair,
We may spend the whole day sitting in a chair.
Our hair can diversify into many styles
So occasionally our creations may be wild.

Ordering food and discussing latest gossip,
Deep diving discussions into politicians' cross-ups.
After we've released the frustration of the day,
We go home calm with hair that slays.

Preparing for a Corporate Job

Sisters, prepare for your corporate interviews.
Wear a straight-hair wig for an accepted view.
Smile at all the interviewer's corny jokes,
Even though he's behaving like an annoying bloke.

Smiling and nodding at him every time,
While using the whitest accent you can find.
Studies show he likes to hire who looks like him,
So, pretend you're white to comfort him.

If you win, a white competitor may discredit you,
They used to say, "Affirmative action hired you."
Affirmative action primarily helped white women,
But it's easier to try to devalue the black woman.

Yes, you're more than qualified for the position,
But you must play against society's biased disposition.
Use the Crown Act to protect you when you get the job;
Ditch the wig and wear an Afro to taunt the snobs.

The Men Who Hate Me

What the Manosphere Detests

What the manosphere detests the most
Is the black woman.
For her strong presence causes jealousy
To his hidden inner woman.

Being a self-reliant black woman,
He equates to her not wanting a man.
His hurt feelings
Must destroy her self-esteem
For her to succumb to his minion clan.

Making her own life's decision
In choosing a man
Angers the manosphere
For control must be in their hands.

The passport bro travels the globe
Singing his hate for the black woman.
He intertwines his need
To find a submissive foreign woman
With boasting his hatred for the black woman.

What the manosphere detests the most
Is the black woman winning.
He spews hate speech out his mouth,
For her name is stuck in his throat as he's grinning.

Asking her,
"What do you bring to the table?"
For a table he doesn't even know how to build.
But what he really wants to say,
Is, "When will you pay my bills?"

If you are a dependent black woman,
He still won't like you.
He'll call you a gold-digger
And then he'll try to stifle you.

Black women,
It doesn't matter what we do.
The manosphere's premise
Is built on the foundation
Of despising you.

Lower Her Standards

"Lower her standards,
Lower her goals.
A black woman
Should do as she's told."

Can't have big dreams.
Can't have big hopes.
Apparently, black women,
You don't deserve
Good horoscopes.

How dare you want a man
Who's equal or higher?
How dare you want a man
Who respects you
And fulfills your desires?

"Lower her standards,
Lower her goals.
A black woman
Should stop being bold."

Can't live your life
Cause undesirable men
Try to control you.
Want you to lower yourself
So they can own you.

Wearing kitten keels
And tapping around.
Men telling black women
How to be a woman
Is the behavior of a clown.

"Lower her standards,
Lower her goals.
A black woman should listen
And stop being cold."

Bed Wench

He called me "a bed wench,"
Because my husband is white.
He told me I'm the old master's
House Negro slave wife.

When a black man
Marries a white wife,
Why are you heathens
Not disrupting his life?

He called me "a bed wench,"
Because I married a white man.
He said my husband is using me
As his slave hand.

If my white husband
Shows me respect and love too,
Why would I want to leave him
For a bully like you?

Am I Not a Woman, Too?

Am I not a woman, too?
Must I be disrespected by you?

Your old racist mind
Has you dehumanizing me every time.
Won't admit your mistake
And an apology cannot be traced.

Am I not a woman, too?
Must I be disrespected by you?

It took another white man
To explain why you're a despicable man.
Head down in shame for being called out,
You retreated into the corner to pout.

Am I not a woman, too?
Must I be disrespected by you?

For you cut in the gap of the line for your wife
Me saying, "Excuse me, sir," is an attack on your life?
Since her protector is not viewed as strong,
The wife said, "Oh, I guess what he did was wrong."

The Hate of Single Black Mothers

The manosphere
Said the single black mother
Is used goods.
While the child's father
They uplift
Even when he's a deadbeat
Living in a broken trailer or in the hood.
The deadbeat
Can have children across all state lines,
The manosphere
Will make him feel he can still shine.
For they are uplifting their brother in crime.

The black manosphere
Said the single black mother
Is used goods.
Angry that another race of man
Married her and treats her good.
Stealing her pictures
From the Internet.
His hurt feelings
Call these successful men
Degenerates.

The manosphere
Said the single black mother
Is used goods.
Wants her to stop being picky
And accept his friend's damaged manhood.
Degrading her to use her,
For when she's winning
He can't abuse her.

Pigeon-Toe Jingle

"And that's why you're single."
This is a pigeon-toe man's jingle.

Every time a single black woman
Disagrees with this narcissistic man,
He seethes his manipulative plan.
Hoping an insecure black woman
Will fall for his brand's jingle,
Overlooking that pigeon-toe is single.

Trying to use the fact
That you're happy and single against you.
And then reeling it in with,
"No man wants you."
This is the resounding anthem
Of the pigeon-toe man.

Forced Submission

He said, "Sisters,
Talk to your husbands
With the same respect as you do
Your white boss."

Why do you assume
My boss is white?
If respect is given,
Reciprocation is only right.

You want us to work
And submit to you?
Bear your children,
Clean, and cook too?

You want biblical submission,
Without giving me a retirement plan.
Stop talking about a white boss
And do your duty as a man.

Let Me Have My Flowers

Can't you just let me
Have my flowers
Without your need
To disempower?

Yes, your way
Is different from mine,
But I have no intentions
Of changing
My creative style at any time.

Must I continue
With this dance
Of humbling myself
To not hurt your ego's stance?

I know you think
Your way is the best
And your manhood
Makes you think
You're better than the rest.

But can't you just let me
Have my flowers
And suppress your need
To disempower?

Violence Against Black Women

Sisters experience
Physical violence at forty percent,
No matter her partner's
Racial descent.

For society has contempt
For the black woman,
A rooted disregard
Against us as women.

Black women make up seven percent
Of the US population;
From all the women killed by partners or exes,
She's thirty percent in the nation.

It doesn't matter
Her status or education,
These are the lines
Drawn to her black station.

Marked Targets

To the men who hate us
And yell venomous words
Against black women,
You're the fuel that adds
To the hate that causes our deaths
In this nation.

Excluding Me

Feminist vs. the Black Woman

In the beginning
Feminist excluded the black woman.
But when they needed numbers
They included the same black women.

Refusing to stand up
For the black woman's plight,
Yet these feminists always want us
To join in on their fights.

Watching the manosphere
Use black women as feminist's fame,
Clearly shows us
We can't trust these two-faced games.

The manosphere degrades
The black woman,
And the feminist group
Protects the white woman.

Malcolm X said it clearly,
The black woman is the least protected.
And you can see it daily
Whenever the manosphere is projected.

So don't come for me,
Talking about you are "one percent black."
Saying we're sisters against the men,
But when it counts, you turn your back.

The Color of My Military Hair

Military's regulations on coloring hair
Exclude the black woman.
For those privileges
Are only held for the white woman.

For you can change your hair color
To any natural shade.
But the only acceptance
Is that you are of the Caucasian shade.

A white woman
With ancestors with only black hair,
Can color her hair
Any spectrum without a care.

The black woman's options
Are dark brown or black.
Even if there are other colors in her DNA
She must choose a color reserved for "Blacks."

No Respect for Rastafarians

Rastafarian religion is not respected,
For even in Corporate America, it's still rejected.
Inclusion is rejected by those already included,
Ignorance of anything outside themselves is rooted.

Rastafarian religion is not respected,
For even in the military, it's still rejected.
Fighting for some accommodation is a waiting game,
For biases of misunderstandings remain the same.

SWAN Against Black Women

Black Weathering is a dismal battle,
That slices through the core of our being.
But using this studied diagnosis as a shield,
SWAN excluded the **Black Woman**
From critical woman research we need.
So, the next time you invite us to the table,
For donations to aide in women's health,
Keep walking towards a place called Hell.

No Black Cliques

"Break it up! Break it up!
No cliques in my military!"

Only cliques are in black skin.
Not allowed initial comfort
From the strange new world
I was thrown in.
Must be a token
In a white girl group,
Or sit alone by myself.
Drill sergeants won't tolerate
An all-black female group,
But somehow the white groups
Are safe havens
Free from being a clique.

The Ban on Natural Hair

My natural hair
Was viewed as unprofessional,
For the military hair regulations
Deemed my hair transgressional.

He said, "Get out of my military
If you don't like the hair rules,
Or just bald your head
Like men in boot camps do."

Balding my head
Is against the regulations.
So, even if you own the military,
Males and females have different obligations.

Jamming dirty rulers
In my TWA hair.
Making sure I don't exceed
The 3-inch bulk rule against big hair.

We're allowed to wear ponytails
During physical training time,
But when I wear an Afro puff
You act like I'm committing a crime.

He said, "My wife is black and she's happy
With her relaxed straightened hair."
So, when exactly did you and your wife
Take ownership of my natural hair?

The relaxer was linked
To fibroids and cancer.
Hefty medical bills
For your idea of a hair enhancer.

A black woman wearing locs
Is a spiritual journey
But before 2021, the military perception
Was that it is unkept and dirty.

Two-strand twists
Was often mistaken for loc'd hair.
Punishment for another protective style
That tames my natural big hair.

He said, "Cornrows
Must be the same width from front to back."
But that's not how our hair works
For it's not as thick in the front and back.

Making hair regulations
That go against the biology of my hair,
Then punishing me
Because your ignorance doesn't care.

It's suggested to cover up
My unkempt hair with a wig.
I guess during field day,
Bugs will have a place to happily dig.

No, I can't just flat iron my hair
To make you happy,
For humidity and water
Will revert it back to being nappy.

He said, "I apologize for the ignorance
From others on your base.
Explain to me how your hair works
So accommodations can be placed."

Destroying the Melanin Skin

Hyperpigmentation
Is exploding all over my face.
The melanocytes are attacking
And multiplying like it's a race!

The skincare industry
Uses ingredients that damage my skin.
They're annoyed by my complaints,
So apparently, I can't win.

The mainstream won't do studies
On melanated skin.
Excluded to use the catchall
That put my skin in the turmoil it's in.

When doctors of color segregate
To teach us proper ingredients and habits,
White girls on YouTube yell, "Racist!"
And behave like rabid rabbits.

Now that our skincare movements
Have disrupted their pockets.
They're adjusting and making slight changes
To placate us with new plakats.

Sister Protection

Fighting to protect my brothers' backs,
Organizing marches and leading the packs.
But when I need my brothers to fight for me,
All I see is my sisters marching next to me.

We are dying off at alarming rates;
Invisible, we disappear without a trace.
Always carrying someone on our backs,
When we need them, it's a disappearing act.

No more caping and saving you,
No more protecting and guiding you.
It's time to protect myself and my sister's back,
Because she's the only one who will protect me back.

Black and Educated

Educated and black:
The black woman
Is winning in that.

For black women
Are the most educated
Demographic
In the United States.
Yet, we have the highest
Unemployment rate.

Betrayal of Me

This Cheating Man

Oh, but look at this cheating man
Who's spreading his seed across the land.
Please, leave him when you can.
He's a destruction to your whole life plan,
For he's a despicable cheating man.

He's in and out of every sheet.
He's breeding up all over the street.
Please hide your daughter from this pest.
He'll turn her life into a mess.

Oh, but look at this cheating man
Who's broker than your frying pan.
He's taking money out of your hand,
To subsidize his cheating plan.
His words are like the sinking sand.

He's in and out of different sheets,
So please throw him back to the streets.
Even if you fell victim to his seed,
Still reclaim the life you want to lead.

Oh, but look at this cheating man
Who's wearing expensive designer brands.
Throwing money at whatever he can.
Unable to control his own weak glands,
And strutting around like a decent man.

He's in and out of various sheets.
This pompous man keeps no receipts.
If he's justifying being a cheater,
He'll eventually become a wife-beater.

Wait 'Til I Catch You in These Streets

Living in luxury in my best friend's house,
All while you're trying to take her spouse.
Pouting and acting like you're so weak;
Wait 'til I catch you in these streets.

Since her man won't protect her peace,
Her bestie is here to make you cease.
Until she wakes up and leaves that cheat,
Wait 'til I catch you in these streets.

Prenup he requested protects her wealth.
Fear of divorce, he now fakes bad health.
You're ducking and hiding under his sheets;
Wait 'til I catch you in these streets.

Since all your morals have gone to hell,
And being a side hen has served you well,
Let me teach you what happens with deceit.
Wait 'til I catch you in these streets.

Bestie finally dumped that worthless man.
Now I can properly implement my plan.
Braiding my Afro so my hair is on fleek,
Wait 'til I catch you in these streets.

Back Stabber

Smiling face
Is looking at me,
Pretending to be my friend
Like I can't see.

Then as soon as I turn
My back,
You race towards me
With a slash attack.

I turned to the side
In time to avert you,
You tripped down the stairs,
Becoming black and blue.

Learned my lesson
From the last time,
So I was fully prepared
For your dutty crime.

Doctor's Betrayal

A doctor-patient relationship
Is a vulnerable thing,
But as a black woman,
It could be a dangerous sting.

When doctors dismiss us
And disregard our pain
Are you surprised
Our death rates have higher gains?

Three times as likely to die from pregnancy
Because of doctors' neglect,
And misdiagnosed with illnesses
When doctor's biases help them to select.

It doesn't matter her socioeconomic status
Or education,
For a black woman,
This is their doctor's negation.

Two in three pregnancy deaths
Are preventable,
But most doctors treat black women
As though we're dispensable.

She said, "On the behalf of all doctors,
I apologize for what you went through.
But rest assured, I will do my duty
As your doctor to help you."

Color of Betrayal

My love for you is no longer there,
For you left betrayals everywhere.
Your betrayal was not physical touch,
It was a damage of emotions and trust.

I shared my precious secrets with you,
And in return, you used them against me.
Making my memories unclassified,
You formed a coalition of hate and lies.

You can't see the darkness in my world,
For you live in a privileged dimension.
You lack empathy for my journey's pain
Because my skin tone is against your norm.

You're enchanted with each touch of my skin,
But that part of me will never again be yours.
For you betrayed the very entity that is me,
So your pleading cannot change my mind.

You Love Me When I'm Gone

You said what you missed the most
When I left
Is never being able
To kiss my full, big lips
While feeling the warmth of my body
In your arms.

But when you had me in your life,
You took me for granted
And treated me with contempt.

Instead of living in your shadow,
I decided to free myself
And to live my full life.

For the Love of Me

I Must Love Me to Love You

The only way to love you
Is to start by loving myself too,
For only when I love myself
Can I reciprocate that love to somebody else.

Loving yourself is a beautiful thing
Because it allows your soul to grow and win.

So, I accept the coils of my nappy hair,
The widening of my hips from the child I'll bear,
The shade of darkness of my melanin skin,
And dismiss self-hate from trapping me within.

Loving yourself is a beautiful thing
Because it allows your heart happiness to sing.

Now that I completely love myself,
I can show true love to someone else.
And now that I finally love myself,
I can decipher who loves me or only themselves.

Love Can Be a Dangerous Thing

Life is a series of the strangest things.
Falling in love with you was a dangerous thing.
Although we fought hard to be together,
Life has beat us down with stormy weather.

Some loves are encapsulated in time,
And some loves are dangerous crimes.
So I step back to evaluate my life,
And make sure I'm not protecting any strife.

I deserve love that is pure and true,
So I must first learn to love myself too.
For when I learn to take better care of my heart,
I will have better armor to protect me from the start.

Being Loved on by My King

Every time you call me, "Queen,"
A happy sensation overflows my being.
And when I softly call you, "King,"
I hear your breath hitch before it sings.

In a world that's cold outside
I'm so happy to have you by my side.
And every time you kiss my melanin skin,
I feel confirmation that in this life, I can win.

Your gentle kiss and warm embrace
Melt slowly into my skin without a trace.
Your love takes my mind off society's hate,
Allowing my worries the space to dissipate.

Feeling at peace in the warmth of your arms
And the security of your protection from harm.
For I love the way you make my heart sing
As I'm being loved on by you, my King.

Sun Kissed Lips

Sun kiss
On my full lips.
I woke up at sunrise
To you kissing me as I opened my eyes.

You secured my bonnet on my hair
And continued to kiss me without a care.
I forgot you messed up my protective style
Because your kissing became provocatively wild.

River of Emotions

My heart is a river filled with raw emotions
That expands as it flows towards the vast ocean.
Overflowing over the edge of the river fall of life,
Drifting to bash into each rock of the current's strife.

Your raft set sail on a quest to catch me,
For you were determined you must protect me.
As you battle the currents of my river of emotions,
You grabbed me in time from being lost in the ocean.

Wiping away the wet coils from my caramel face.
You wrapped your arms around me, so I felt safe.
This newest of feelings gives me a sense of calm.
No longer alone weathering rapid rivers and storms.

Not Alone in This Bias World

Can you listen to the beat of my heart?
Then you'll know how I felt from the start.
No misunderstandings or careless mistakes.
Let the rhyme take their discord's place.

Living in a world unprotected,
Evil wants to see me rejected.
Can't let them win in this life;
Must always dodge their knives.

Can you listen to the song in my soul?
Together our love makes me whole.
Wrapping me in your arms so close,
The safety of your arms is like a drug dose.

Living in a world that's so biased,
My annoyance is maxed to the highest.
You in my world, makes me calm.
You've got my heart in your palm.

Can you listen to the tone of my being?
The sound of your baritone is freeing.
Serenity fills my coffee chest
As adrenaline fights upcoming quests.

I Only Hear Your Voice

In a world filled with the haze of blurry faces,
Yours is the only vivid face I can clearly see.
Muzzled voices of chaotic sounds,
Yours is the only voice that soothes my soul.

Watching you from behind my messy Fro,
Not realizing the state of my outer appearance.
Mesmerized by your swagger as you draw near,
You pulled me into your arms and held me tight.

Pressing your lips against mine.
Oh, the surreal sweetness of your kiss.
You pulled away and whispered gently,
"Babe, let's go get your hair done."

Love Request

You are a blessing sent from above,
A prayer whispered from my mother's lips.
Blown down to me to melt my heart,
Her love is encapsulated in this request.

"You're not alone, my dear daughter.
Mama didn't leave you unprotected.
Open up your heart to his love,
And accept this prayer I requested."

I defiantly hid from his love,
But my walls started crumbling with each kiss,
And that's how he tricked my melting heart,
For he already made me his destiny's quest.

Love Is Like Magic

Every time I see you, it's like magic;
A blessing from above, I feel panicked.
I can't believe you're in my life
And that I'm going to be your wife.

For when I'm by your side, I'm dramatic;
A blessing from above, it's like magic.
I can't believe you're in my life;
I just can't wait to be your wife.

Hmm, let the rivers and mountains
Harmonize for us two.
Let the stars in heaven sprinkle down
And bless us too.
This reality is true.

For every time I see you, it's like magic;
A blessing from above, my heart's erratic.
I can't believe you're in my life
And that I'm going to be your wife.

When I'm by your side, we're fanatics;
A blessing from above, it's like magic.
I can't believe you're in my life;
I'm finally going to be your wife.

Hmm, there was a time and place
When our future seemed so bleak.
Got me questioning my faith
And my body becoming weak.
That's when it piqued.

For when I look at you, it's like magic;
A blessing from above, it's climatic.
I can't believe you're in my life
And now it's time to be your wife.

You got me in your arms; I'm ecstatic;
You're blessing from above; I'm black girl magic.
I can't believe you're in my life
And that I am your awesome wife.

Love the Skin You're In

Love your beautiful
Sun-kissed skin.
Love the vibrant shades
Of brown you're in.
Gradient tones of Mother Earth.

Love the bends and swirls
Of all your coils.
Love the waves and twirls
Of all your curls.
Hair spiraling upwards to the sky.

Love all the curves of you
Love the hourglass variants
From small to big bums
And slender to wider hips.
The shapes of the black woman.

Love the medium
To the fullness
Of your plump berry sweet lips.
Giving the iconic black woman's
Full-blown kiss.

So let others' feelings get hurt
When you express love for yourself.
For black girl magic
Needs you
To love the skin you're in.

From the Author

Hi, I'm Daniella M. Butler, the author of *In Her Skin: The Black Woman*. My book is an expression of various experiences as a black woman in America, with stories representing our different hues. I hope you enjoyed it.

Black women are not monolith. We have shared and individualized experiences. However, it's our unique experiences that stem from our blackness combined with our womanhood that led me to write this poetry book. Obviously, I can't write about everything in our journey, but this is a start. This book is my second published poetry book in the *Unsilenced Voices* series. The first was *Her Stolen Tears: Release of Emotions*.

You can find me on most social media platforms such as BlueSky Social, YouTube, etc. via @daniellambutler. My Facebook handle is @daniellambutlerauthor.

Upcoming Books
Soul's Urge: Love's Rebirth (novel)
Children of Time (YA book series)
Where Is Frisky? (children's book)
And more...

www.ingramcontent.com/pod-product-compliance
Lightning Source LLC
Chambersburg PA
CBHW060345050426

42449CB00011B/2846

www.ingramcontent.com/pod-product-compliance
Lightning Source LLC
Chambersburg PA
CBHW060345050426

42449CB00011B/2846